INDIA TO THE RESCUE

INDIA TO THE RESCUE

SUSHANT SINGH

WITH

SHRUTHI RAO

Illustrated by Shagnik Chakraborty

JUGGERNAUT BOOKS
C-I-128, First Floor, Sangam Vihar, Near Holi Chowk,
New Delhi 110080, India

First published by Juggernaut Books 2021

10 9 8 7 6 5 4 3 2 1

P-ISBN: 9789391165000
E-ISBN: 9789391165031

Typeset in Adobe Caslon Pro by R. Ajith Kumar, Noida

Printed at Thomson Press India Ltd

WARNING: THIS IS NOT A WORK OF FICTION!

India has a large armed force but it mostly guards our borders. You'll hear about our military operations fighting Pakistan and China in the north but our other missions tend to be rare and not spoken of.

This is the story of the time when the island country of the Maldives, which lies in the Indian Ocean near Sri Lanka, was attacked in the dead of night. India flew to its rescue in one of the most daring operations in our history – Operation Cactus. It was one of our country's quickest, boldest and most successful missions!

This account was originally written by Sushant Singh, who researched the story and interviewed many of the characters in it. I've adapted it, adding a few extra dialogues and dramatizing some scenes. But be warned – every detail in this book is real!

Shruthi Rao

HOW TO TAKE OVER A COUNTRY IN 10 SIMPLE STEPS

1. Choose your country. The smaller and more peace-loving it is, the better.
2. Get a partner in crime. Are they: Familiar with the country? Check. Hungry for power? Check. Rolling in money? You've hit the jackpot!
3. Build your army. Use the money (from point 2) to buy arms and ammunition and pay mercenaries (soldiers for hire).
4. Plan the takeover down to the smallest detail: speed and secrecy is of the essence.
5. Attack at night or dawn when defences are low.
6. Seize the country's transport and communication networks. Close all roads, rail links, ports and airports. Take over television, radio, telephones, cell towers and the media.
7. Destroy the military and capture their arsenal.
8. Arrest political and military leaders.
9. Create a ruckus on the streets to cow down residents.
10. Announce that you're the new leader.

Congratulations! You're now the head of a country.

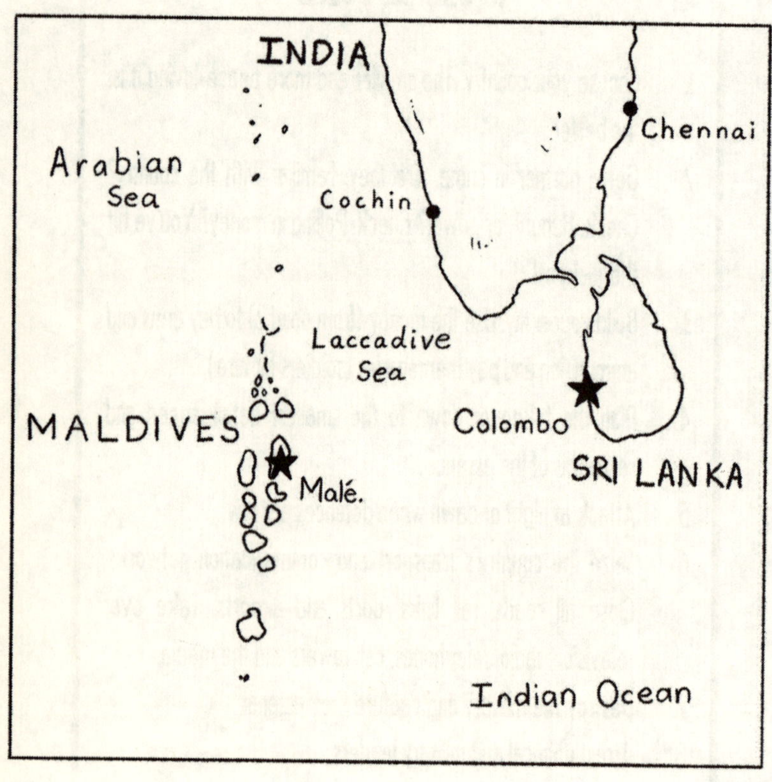
INDIA
Chennai
Arabian
Sea
Cochin
Laccadive
Sea
MALDIVES
Colombo
Malé.
SRI LANKA
Indian Ocean

WHERE IS THE MALDIVES?

The Maldives is an archipelago made up of 1,200 tiny islands. You can walk around the tiniest one in under five minutes. The island of Malé is just twice the size of Bangalore's Lalbagh, or a little more than five times the size of Delhi's Lodi Gardens!

The Maldivian islands are in the shape of a garland, which is probably where it got its name from: mala (garland) + dweepa (island).

MALÉ UNDER ATTACK

MALÉ, MALDIVES

3 November 1988

It was just before dawn. All was quiet in Malé, the capital city of the Maldives. But scary things were afoot.

In the dark, a large ship had quietly sailed close to the coast. Two speedboats left the ship, whizzed through the waters and landed on the jetty. Moments later, dozens of men sprang out of the boats, machine guns in their hands.

The shadowy figures swept through the city. They headed towards government buildings and took their positions.

And then it began.

The rat-tat-tat of machine guns and the boom of grenades shattered the silence of the dawn. Malé was under attack.

At the presidential palace, President Maumoon Abdul Gayoom woke up with a jolt. In no time, his security team whisked him out of the palace and to a safe house. Only the most trusted people knew of its location. The President was safe – for now.

The attackers captured the television and radio stations. They cut off the water and electricity supplies to the city.

They opened fire on the headquarters of the National Security Service (NSS), the organization responsible for maintaining the peace and security of the country. The soldiers there fought back bravely but could not overpower the attackers. The NSS soldiers were now stuck inside the building, surrounded by the attackers.

The Maldivians were outnumbered and outclassed. The country was in desperate need of help.

SOS! SOS!

DOES A COUNTRY REALLY NEED A MILITARY?

As long as you have unsteady relationships with your neighbours, a military is necessary for any country to protect itself. Large countries spend tonnes of money on a strong defence force.

On the other hand, many small countries, especially island nations that mind their own business, get along just fine without a military. But what if other busybodies don't let them live in peace? Valid question. Some of these small countries have pacts and protection agreements with larger countries for just this kind of scenario.

The Maldives' NSS at the time that our story unfolds was a small organization that looked after the safety and security of the people. It was made up of the local police, a two-plane air force, coastguards and so on. But after the 1988 attack, the Maldives built up its defences and now the better-equipped Maldives National Defence Force protects the country.

NEW DELHI

6 a.m.

Arun Banerjee, the Indian High Commissioner to the Maldives, was sleeping comfortably wrapped up in a quilt. He was enjoying a short break in New Delhi.

But the insistent ring of the telephone cut through his sleep. Who could it be at this hour?

Arun sat up groggily and reached for the phone.

'Hello?'

The call was from his secretary in Malé. 'Mr Banerjee!' he said. 'Malé is under attack!'

'What!' Arun was wide awake now. He listened, stunned, as the secretary filled him in on all the details.

'The Maldives needs help, Mr Banerjee. President Gayoom has sent out SOS messages to India, Pakistan, Malaysia, even the UK and US. Can India help?'

India could. As the largest country in South Asia, India wanted to establish itself as a regional superpower. It was already active in operations with Sri Lanka.

Arun hung up and hurriedly placed a call to India's Ministry of External Affairs (MEA). They were already neck-deep in action. They'd heard the news and directed the Indian Air Force (IAF) to prepare for a mission to the Maldives. The IAF chiefs had sent orders for aircraft and officers to be on standby and wait for further instructions.

The MEA briefed the Prime Minister of

India, Rajiv Gandhi, who called for an urgent high-level meeting.

WHAT WAS ARUN'S JOB?

Countries have set-ups called foreign ministries, with officials whose job is to work with foreign officials of other countries. That's how countries conduct business and discussions with each other.

India's foreign ministry (also called the Ministry of External Affairs, or MEA) sent Arun to live and work in the Maldives and be India's representative there.

Usually, people like Arun are called ambassadors and they work in embassies. But India's ambassadors to the Commonwealth countries (countries that were once part of the British empire) are called high commissioners. That was what Arun was, and the office he worked at was known as the Indian High Commission.

SOUTH BLOCK, NEW DELHI

8.30 a.m.

The South Block in Delhi is home to the Prime Minister's Office (PMO) and the Ministry of Defence and the MEA. Arun got there quickly and headed to the Army Operations Room. It was buzzing with activity. The who's who of the country were in that room – bigwigs from India's government, foreign ministry and the military.

Prime Minister Rajiv Gandhi walked in, and the meeting began.

Nobody knew anything about what was

happening in Malé. Who were these rebels? How many of them were there? What weapons were they armed with? Did they have any backup or help?

Everybody had questions. Nobody had answers.

How could they proceed with absolutely no information on hand? Even then, amid all the chaos and noise, a plan took shape.

One thing was certain – this operation would involve all three branches of the military.

The army would lead the operation, because the best place to gain control over the enemy is on land. The air force would fly the troops over to the Maldives. They would also bring other supplies, like arms, food, medicines and vehicles. And since the Maldives was an island nation, the navy would be on alert, ready to assist.

But which brigade of the army would they send in?

'That's an easy decision,' said the army chiefs. 'The Para Brigade.'

There was a chorus of 'Yes!' and 'Of course!' around the room.

Arun slowly nodded to himself. Of course. It made perfect sense. The aircraft of the IAF might not be able to land in the Maldives at all. They would need paratroopers, soldiers who could parachute down into the thick of the action. The daredevil Paras would be ideal for such an operation.

THE REAL-LIFE SUPERHEROES

The 50th Parachute Brigade, or Para Brigade, is a part of the Special Forces of the Indian Army. They are also known simply as the Paras.

Paras are trained to jump off aircraft with parachutes on their backs and descend into enemy-occupied land. Besides, they are aces in ground combat. When they find themselves in a tight spot, these daring soldiers make quick decisions and take swift action, which is why they were the right choice for this operation.

But wait, what is a brigade?

A brigade is a major tactical military formation, headed by a Brigadier, in this case, Farooq Bulsara.

A brigade is made up of battalions. In the Para Brigade, there were about 900 men in each battalion. 3 Para and 6 Para were battalions, officially known as the 3rd Battalion and 6th Battalion of the Para Brigade.

Each battalion in the Para Brigade was made up of companies; each company had 160 men.

A company was further split into platoons, with about 32 men each.

PARA BRIGADE HEADQUARTERS, AGRA

10 a.m.

While the bigwigs made plans for the Para Brigade, the Paras themselves were blissfully unaware of what was in store for them. Their department was preparing for an inspection. They were only focused on how to impress the inspectors.

Out of the blue, Major Vinod Bhatia of the Para Brigade got an urgent call from one of the officers at the South Block meeting. 'There's going to be an island operation; a hundred paratroopers have to prepare for a beach assault. Wait for further info.'

Vinod assumed the operation was for Sri Lanka. He pulled out the maps and aerial photographs of Sri Lanka and spread them out on the table.

Forty minutes later, Vinod got another call. This time it was the Vice Chief of Army Staff, who spoke briskly. 'The operation is in the Maldives. Get one battalion of paratroopers ready to fly by afternoon. The rest of the Para Brigade will move at night.'

Wait, what?

'But, sir,' said Vinod. 'Not even one battalion is available in full strength. How–'

The Vice Chief cut him off. 'How dare you question my orders! I'll charge you with insubordination!'

Vinod gulped. Message received. This was serious.

He hung up and cleared the Sri Lanka maps from the table. But maps of the Maldives? Where would he get those from?

He called two of his officers. 'Bring me maps of the Maldives.'

'From where, sir?'

'Anywhere! Hotels, tourist bureaus – get me brochures, maps, anything! Go go go!'

As the officers hurried away, Brigadier Farooq Bulsara entered the room. Farooq was the Commanding Officer (CO) of the Para Brigade. He was an energetic and flamboyant man; when he entered a room, he filled it with his forceful personality. He lived up to his nickname – Bull.

As Vinod informed Farooq of the developments, Farooq raised his hand.

'I have just one question,' he said.

'Yes?'

'Where in the blazes is the Maldives?'

Farooq, Vinod and other officers of the Para Brigade were huddled together in a discussion.

'Let 6 Para lead the operation,' said Farooq.

'But two companies of 6 Para are guarding the COD,' said Vinod.

The COD, or Central Ordnance Depot, was where weapons and ammunition of the army were stored.

'So we'll have to get them to release the companies,' said Farooq.

The CO of 6 Para placed a call to the COD.

The COD refused. 'Can't be done,' they said. 'Not at such short notice.'

'We need them for an operation,' said the CO.

'Impossible,' said the COD.

'Then they'll have to shoot their way through and come join us!' shot back the CO.

It worked. 6 Para was soon on its way.

3.30 P.M.

The meeting at the Para Brigade headquarters was as highly charged as the one at South Block a few hours earlier. Everyone shouted over each other. Farooq shook his head. 'Compared to this, a fish market can be called serene,' he said.

Arun Banerjee, who was also at this meeting, laughed. After the meeting at South Block, army officers had carted Arun off to Agra. Arun had brought with him a coffee-table book on the Maldives and a photo album with ten photographs of Malé. The other officers had with them tourist

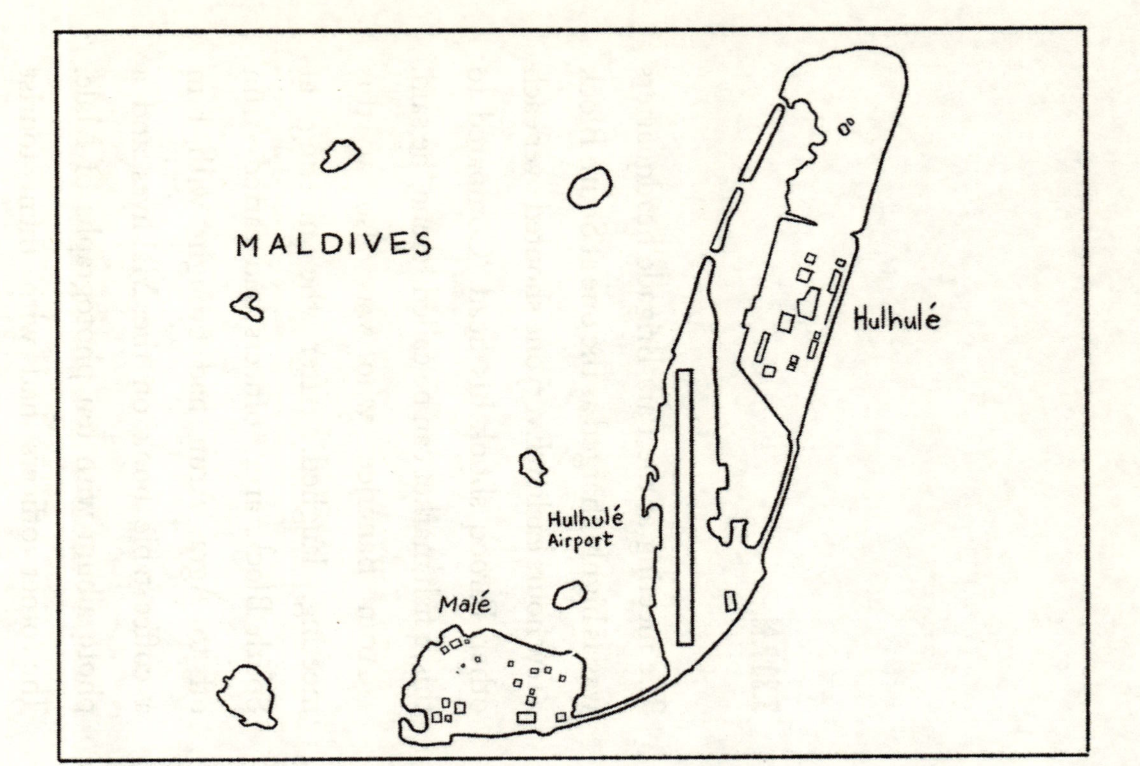
MALDIVES
Hulhulé
Hulhulé Airport
Malé

maps and sketches of Malé, the island capital, and Hulhulé, the island next to Malé. The international airport was at Hulhulé.

A military operation based on these papers? Arun grimaced, as the discussions proceeded.

How would they land at Malé? That was the main problem.

One option was for the soldiers to be paradropped from an aircraft on to Malé, where they could take out the rebels.

'But is there a large enough DZ?' asked one of the officers.

DZ meant dropping zone, the area where the paratroopers would land.

Farooq looked at the maps and shook his head. 'We need a DZ as large as a dozen football fields put together. Doesn't look like Malé has much open space.'

'That's true, it doesn't,' confirmed Arun.

'Imagine the paratroopers landing in the sea!'

Farooq said. 'Tied to the parachute harness, loaded with the weight of the parachute as well as their weapons! They'll never make it to the land. They'll sink like stones!'

There was silence as the officers weighed their options.

One of the IAF officers cleared his throat.

'Yes?' said Farooq.

'There's another problem,' said the IAF officer. 'We have only sixty D5 parachutes packed and ready. We'll send the rest later.'

'Later?' exploded Farooq. 'There is no later!'

He paced around the room. 'That would mean that even if the full strength of 160 men is on the flight, only sixty will be in the initial part of the mission!'

'Any other options?' asked another officer.

'We could land at Hulhulé airport,' said Farooq. 'We can take control of it. Then we can get boats and use the sea to go to Malé.'

'But isn't the airport under the control of the rebels?' asked an officer.

'No,' said Farooq. 'A Maldivian minister has been in touch with the PMO. The airport is still safe.'

'And if the rebels capture it by the time we get there?'

'We'll tie up with the Air Traffic Control (ATC) for a password or signal. We'll make sure it's safe before we land,' said Farooq.

And what if it's not safe? The unasked question hung in the air.

Sketchy plans. Not enough men. The chances of success didn't look too good.

THE WRONG MAP AND THE RIGHT PLAN

Arun was the only one in the entire operation who had been to the Maldives and knew the country first-hand. He was in great demand. First, the army bombarded him with questions. After they were done, the air force whisked him away to another room. They spread out a large map of an airport on the table and asked Arun questions about it.

Arun placed his hands on the map and examined it. He frowned. Something was wrong. He narrowed his eyes as his gaze ran across the map. And then he got it.

'Wrong map!' he shouted, banging it with a fist.

The officers froze.

'This is the map of Gan airport!' he said. 'Hundreds of kilometres away from Malé! We need the map of Hulhulé airport.'

Some officers hurriedly pushed away the map, while some others scurried to get the right one.

Phew! What a relief that Arun had noticed the mistake. However, at the same time, he couldn't help but feel a niggle of worry.

What complete lack of information for such a major international venture!

Meanwhile, Farooq briefed his brigade.

'This is the plan,' he said. 'Phase one. We will fly to the Maldives, land at Hulhulé airport and secure it. If Hulhulé is under rebel control, we'll airdrop sixty soldiers who'll try to overpower the rebels.' Farooq paused. 'And I'll jump along with them.'

'Me too,' said Vinod. Farooq nodded.

The other officers exchanged surprised looks. The Brigade Commander and his main officer jumping with the first team? Unheard of! But they should've expected it. Farooq was a daredevil.

'Phase two,' said Farooq. 'A company of 6 Para will get into a boat, go over to Malé and locate and rescue President Gayoom.'

He continued, 'Phase three: The IAF will fly in more planes and bring in more soldiers. We'll build up military strength in Malé and Hulhulé. Phase four: Get the President to safety and mop up the rebels.'

This sounded like a solid plan. It was good to have something concrete to work with.

KHERIA AIR BASE, AGRA

Afternoon

No. 44 Squadron, under Wing Commander Anant Bewoor, got IL-76 aircraft ready to fly the paratroopers to the Maldives.

6 Para would board one plane, along with sixty D5 parachutes. The other IL-76 would carry one company of 3 Para of 160 men.

Both ILs would fly directly from Agra to Hulhulé and remain on the ground with engines running while the soldiers got down. Then they would immediately take off and fly to Trivandrum. So both aircraft had to be loaded with enough fuel to last the entire trip.

There was a hustle and bustle on the tarmac the entire afternoon. Trucks and jeeps surged past, with troops carrying arms and equipment. The COs shouted instructions. Fuel trucks

whizzed by. The ILs guzzled fuel. The ground crew made frantic checks. The air crew signed manifests and forms as they rushed from one aircraft to the other.

MEET 44 SQUADRON: THE INDIAN ARMY'S DO-GOODERS

This is a unit of the Indian Air Force, or IAF. When you need someone to ferry and airdrop troops, supplies and equipment, you turn to 44 Squadron. Sometimes they help in other operations too: for instance, they fought in the 1965 and 1971 wars against Pakistan.

And yes, they're great at helping with disaster relief! They make sorties to airdrop relief materials to areas inaccessible by land and rail. A sortie is one trip by an aircraft, usually with a specific mission.

44 Squadron has flown to Sri Lanka and Indonesia during the tsunami, rescued avalanche victims in Kashmir and helped in earthquake-affected areas as well.

Preparations were in full swing. But Farooq was worried.

Will we find boats at Hulhulé? Will we find boatmen? What if we're forced to airdrop soldiers? What if they get hurt?

But he couldn't dwell on these thoughts. He turned his attention to Arun, who was planning to head back home.

'No, no, Arun,' said Farooq. 'You can't leave now. You have first-hand knowledge of the area. You've got to come with us.'

'But my work here is done,' said Arun. 'My role ends just as yours begins.'

'I don't agree,' said Farooq. 'This is a military-cum-political operation. You're still a part of this.'

'I'll just get in the way,' said Arun. 'I'm not a military professional.'

Farooq scoffed at that. 'But you *think* like a military professional.'

Arun was adamant.

Farooq placed a hand on Arun's shoulder. 'Arun,' he said, 'we all have to serve our country, in our own way.'

Arun thought about Farooq's words. He knew Farooq was right.

'All right,' Arun said. 'But I have two conditions.'

'Name them.'

'You have to get permission from the MEA for me to join you.'

'Okay,' said Farooq. 'And?'

'I need a razor.'

'A what?'

'I always start my morning with a shave. I cannot bear to think of starting tomorrow without one.'

Farooq laughed. 'Done,' he said.

So into the IL-76s strode the brave paratroopers, maroon berets on their heads, parachute insignia on their uniforms. They were armed with assault rifles and weapons. And along with them walked the mild-mannered Arun, dressed in civilian clothes. But he was armed too – with a shaving kit, toothbrush and towel.

SOME VERY COOL AIRPLANES

Ilyushin is a Russian design and aircraft manufacturing company. They supplied a bunch of really cool aircraft to India.

The two main carriers were IL-76s. They were originally designed to deliver heavy machinery to remote areas. But militaries around the world adapted them for other uses too, including – hold your breath – to refuel aircraft mid-air!

In India, the IL-76 was called Gajraj. It can carry oversized heavy items (in our story, it carried jeeps along with soldiers). In fact, to stick to the Gajraj theme, let's put it this way – a Gajraj can carry about twenty elephants!

It can land and take off on unpaved, short runways and operate in extreme weather. So it's great for evacuations, urgent war requirements and disaster relief.

The IL-76 was made as a replacement for Antonov AN-12, an aircraft used for carrying cargo. The

AN-12 features in our story too, along with AN-32, another sturdy aircraft. Both these were made by Antonov, a Ukrainian aircraft manufacturing company. All these aircraft conducted sorties to the Maldives that night, bringing in soldiers and equipment.

The Mil Mi-8 helicopter, which ferried our soldiers across islands, is one of the most popular choppers in the world, mainly produced by Russia. It is a transport copter, but mount weapons on it, and it can turn into a gunship!

The Dassault Mirage 2000 was a sleek French fighter jet, very agile and easy to manoeuvre. Just the right machines to strike terror into the hearts of the bad guys in our story.

AGRA

A little before 5 p.m.

All troops and equipment were loaded and final checks completed. The ATC gave them the green signal.

The two IL-76s taxied to the runway and picked up speed. As the sun dipped behind the Taj Mahal, the aircraft took to the skies.

'Chhatri Mata ki jai!' shouted the paratroopers. Victory to the Parachute Goddess!

Operation Cactus was on.

EVERYTHING YOU WANT TO KNOW ABOUT PARACHUTES!

During Operation Cactus, the Paras used Russian-made D5 parachutes.

At that time, most conventional parachutes needed what were called static lines and D-bags, or deployment bags, that helped them deploy, or open up. One end of a cord (static line) was attached to the aircraft. The other end was tied to the D-bag that contained the parachute of the parachutist. The parachutist wore this bag on his or her back. Once the parachutist jumped, the cord became taut. It pulled the D-bag, and the parachute canopy opened up. Then the parachutist glided down. This was to make him or her stable, or else the parachutist would spiral out of control as soon as he or she jumped out.

These parachutes have a disadvantage. They need two or more people to pull the cords back into the aircraft. Besides, the aircraft had to slow down before anybody could jump out.

But Russian D5 parachutes had a drogue stabilizer chute. Basically, a parachute on a parachute. So once the parachutist jumped, a tiny drogue parachute would open up first and help the jumper stabilize or become steady, rather than whirl round and round in the air. Once the parachutist was stable, he or she could pull a cord to deploy the main parachute and then descend.

The advantage was, of course, that they could jump out of speeding aircraft and also jump from high altitudes.

IN THE AIR

Between 5 p.m. and 9 p.m.

The aircraft climbed to their cruising altitudes and commenced level flight.

It was only now that Arun dwelled on the enormity of the situation. They were on their way to a foreign country on a military operation. There were more things that were uncertain than certain. Yet, he could see no fear anywhere in the aircraft. Rather, there was a sense of calm.

Farooq briefed the paratroopers about their task. He passed around Arun's now well-thumbed coffee-table book. The soldiers looked carefully at the photographs and maps of Malé and the pictures of President Gayoom.

After the briefing, Farooq eased himself into a comfortable deckchair, took off his maroon beret and settled down for–

'A nap?' Arun blurted out in surprise. 'Now?'

Farooq raised his index finger. 'If you don't sleep when you get the opportunity, you'll be exhausted.' He turned around and found a comfortable position. 'And if you want to be effective in battle, you should make sure you aren't sleepy.'

He closed his eyes.

The aircraft flew through the skies, passed over south India, and then over the Indian Ocean.

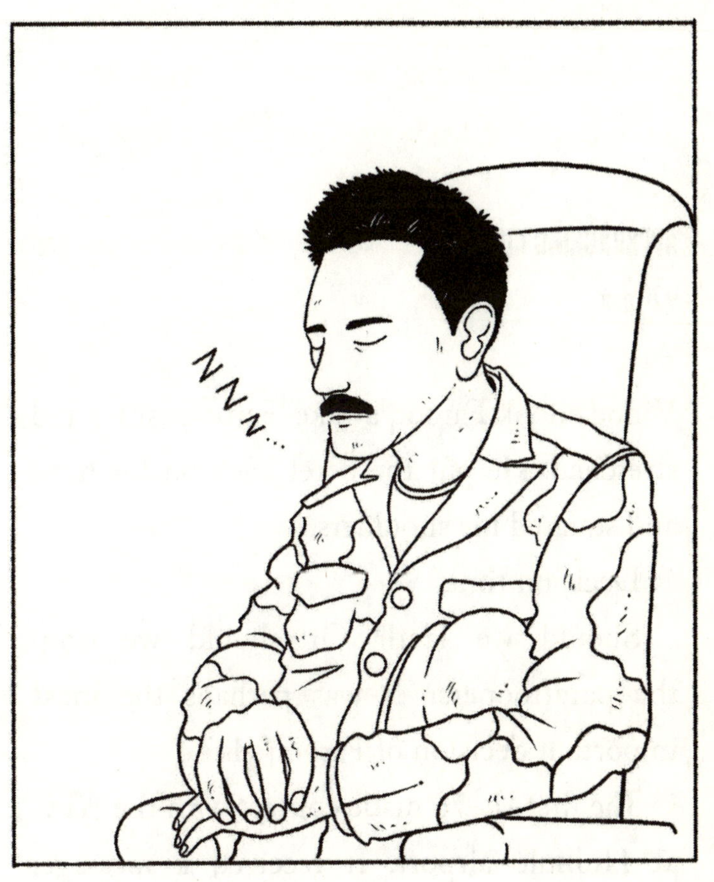
NNN...

APPROACHING HULHULÉ

9.20 p.m.

Vinod shook Farooq awake. Farooq sat up and stretched. He put the beret back on his head and squared his shoulders.

Decision time.

Should we land? Or should we drop the paratroopers? It was perhaps the most important decision of Farooq's life.

The first IL-76 made contact with the ATC at Hulhulé airport. It received a message: Hudiya. That was the password! It meant, quite aptly, guide to the righteous path.

The pilot, Anant Bewoor, gave Farooq a thumbs up. 'Hulhulé is still under government control,' said Anant. 'It's safe to land.'

'How do we know?' asked Farooq. 'What if the rebels are pointing a gun at the head of the ATC official? What if he's being forced to say that it's all safe?'

Vinod nodded. 'We can never be sure,' he said.

'If we land,' said Farooq, 'and the rebels roll a truck filled with explosives over the runway in front of the aircraft right after touchdown, then . . .'

His words lingered in the air.

Then . . . that would be the end of everyone on the aircraft.

'What shall I do?' asked Anant.

This was the moment of truth. And the truth was that there was no way of knowing. Farooq was aware that he held everyone's lives in the palm of his hand.

He closed his eyes for a moment, and then said, 'Go in and land.'

Anant focused on landing. It wasn't an easy task. A tiny runway. On a minuscule island. In the middle of the vast ocean. Completely dark. No runway lights. To make matters worse, the radar picked up a massive echo because of the coral sea surrounding the island. But the IL-76's navigation computer guided the aircraft to align with the runway.

At about 200 metres above sea level, it was time for the second signal. Anant transmitted the message 'Lights' to the ATC. As agreed, the runway lights came on. But just for ten seconds.

Ten seconds was all Anant had to make this landing. He flared out, chopped power and touched down. The runway lights went out.

HULHULÉ INTERNATIONAL AIRPORT, MALDIVES

9.48 a.m.

The men in the aircraft held their breaths as the IL roared down the pitch-dark runway and came to a stop.

Farooq peered out of the window. Everything seemed quiet.

So far so good.

No time to lose. The aircraft had to be emptied out quickly for take-off, so that the second aircraft could land. They lowered the aft-end ramp of the IL. One hundred and fifty men and two jeeps were out in a jiffy.

The soldiers fanned out and headed to their assigned destinations and tasks.

One of the brigadiers who was on the IL turned to Arun. 'I'm going back. Would you like to return with me?'

This time Arun did not hesitate. 'I'll stay,' he said. 'My work is not done yet.'

Within ten minutes, the first IL took off and the second one landed. The soldiers jumped out quickly. They secured the ATC, the jetty and the airfield.

Hulhulé was safe and in the control of the Indian military.

One phase down. Three to go.

It had been sixteen hours since the first phone call for help from the Maldives. It was time for action.

ATC, HULHULÉ

After 10 p.m.

The sound of gunfire and the thud of explosives echoed in the distance. Farooq and Arun crept through tall grass and headed to the ATC.

The Maldivian official who had transmitted the password and switched on the runway lights greeted them. He made contact with the President at his safe house and handed the phone to Arun.

Arun knew the President well. He'd even played cricket with him a few times. He greeted the President and passed the phone to Farooq.

'Mr President,' said Farooq. 'We got your message, and we're here. We'll come and get you.'

'Please hurry up!' said the President. 'The rebels are all around my safe house. I can hear firing close by.'

'We'll do our best,' said Farooq.

That was all he said to the President, but after he hung up, Farooq quipped to Arun, 'I'm not about to go through what I have in these past ten hours, having flown 3,000 kilometres, to lose him to a bunch of ragtag mercenaries!'

Arun stepped out of the ATC and stopped short at seeing some men gathered around it. A jolt of fear shot through Arun. But as one of them stepped into the light, Arun breathed a sigh of relief. They were Maldivian NSS officials. He'd seen them at the President's office and the Ministry of Foreign Affairs.

They too recognized Arun and broke into

wide smiles as they realized that help was here. They hastened to arrange for dhonis from Hulhulé jetty to take the soldiers to Malé. Some of them stepped forward to act as boatmen and guides themselves.

'What luck!' said Farooq. 'Hulhulé is safe, dhonis are available. And thanks to you, we have boatmen and guides!' Farooq clapped Arun on the back. 'And you thought you'd get in the way!'

SO WHAT EXACTLY ARE DHONIS? AND NO, THE ANSWER ISN'T RELATED TO CRICKET!

People have been living on these islands for centuries. How did they get from one island to another?

They used dhonis.

Nope, not the former captain of the Indian cricket team. Dhonis are small handcrafted boats. (If you speak Kannada, Telugu or other south Indian languages, you would've recognized the word in a trice!)

Dhonis originally were sailboats, but now they are motorized.

A speedboat on the other hand, the kind that the terrorists used to get to Malé from the ship, is a motorboat that has a powerful engine and a body designed for high speed. They are the ones you see whizzing by, with a gushing spray of water in their wake, in adrenaline-fuelled movie chases.

The Maldives is moving with the times. Since 2018, the swanky new Sinamalé Bridge connects Malé and Hulhulé, and has made it easy for residents to zoom up and down in no time at all.

HULHULÉ JETTY

It was time for the rescue team to leave. A company of 6 Para under Major R.J.S. Dhillon set out with an NSS guide.

At the same time, a pretend rescue team set out too: a platoon of 3 Para jumped into two boats and headed straight ahead to the main jetty at Malé. The plan was to trick and distract the rebels and prevent them from noticing the real rescue team.

The plan worked beautifully. As the boats went close to the jetty, the rebels opened fire on them.

The soldiers didn't need a second invitation. They'd been waiting for this moment for ten hours.

All guns blazed as they rained bullets on the rebels.

MALÉ, BEACHHEAD

3–4 November, midnight

Dhillon's party landed safely in Malé at another jetty. The rebels were busy with the fake team. Dhillon's men faced no opposition. The soldiers jumped off the boats.

Some of the soldiers established a beachhead, a safe, strong position on a beach in enemy territory from where they could launch an attack inland. The boatmen set off again. They guided the empty boats back to Hulhulé to bring more soldiers to Malé.

Under the cover of darkness, the NSS guide led Dhillon and the rescue team to the home of a Maldivian minister. The minister sent another guide who led them to the President's safe house.

At last!

But it wasn't over yet.

The President's security guards were jittery. They did not trust Dhillon and his party and

refused to let them in. Dhillon tried to convince them, but they didn't budge.

'It's been half an hour,' Dhillon told Farooq over his radio device. 'They're not letting us in.'

'Time is running out! And so is my patience,' muttered Farooq. 'Just shoot your way in if you have to!'

But just then, thankfully, sense prevailed. The guards relented and let them through.

PRESIDENT'S SAFE HOUSE

4 November, 9.48 a.m.

The Indian Army entered the safe house. The President welcomed them with open arms.

'You're safe now, Mr President,' said Dhillon.

'Thank you,' said the President, shaking hands with the officers, tears of relief in his eyes.

Two phases down, two to go.

'Let's move to Hulhulé, Mr President,' Dhillon said.

'No,' said the President. 'Take me to the NSS headquarters.'

NSS HEADQUARTERS

The NSS headquarters was still under siege.

While some officers stayed back in the safe house to guard the President, Dhillon and his forces stormed the NSS headquarters.

They took the mercenaries completely by surprise. A heavy firefight followed. The staccato of machine guns and the sound of grenades rent the air.

The Indian Army overpowered the mercenaries and took control of the NSS headquarters.

WHO ATTACKED THE MALDIVES – AND WHATEVER FOR?

You're probably wondering who these rebels were, right? The attackers belonged to a group called the People's Liberation Organization of Tamil Eelam, or PLOTE, headed by Uma Maheswaran. He was originally part of the Liberation Tigers of Tamil Eelam, or LTTE. This was a group of people unhappy with the policies of the governments against Sri Lankan Tamils. They wanted to set up a separate state of Tamil Eelam within Sri Lanka. Uma Maheswaran split from the LTTE and created PLOTE.

Abdullah Luthufi was a Maldivian expat and businessman who raised chickens on a farm in Sri Lanka. Uma Maheswaran asked him to attack the Maldives. Luthufi funded, recruited, armed and trained the mercenaries.

What exactly were these men after? Power? A base for smuggling operations? Something else? We're not entirely sure.

ACROSS THE MALDIVES

Night of 3–4 November

The IAF aircraft flew up and down from India – they made sixty sorties that night. IL-76s, AN-32s and AN-12s brought in the rest of the Para Brigade and an army field hospital.

A number of Mi-8 helicopters had also arrived. They ferried troops who chased the fleeing rebels across islands. Mirage 2000 fighter aircraft flew low over the islands. It was a show of force, designed to terrorize the rebels.

Many of the rebels surrendered.

Three phases down, one to go.

But there was a new problem. Some of the rebels, including their leader Abdullah Luthufi, took hostages and hurriedly climbed aboard their ship, *MV Progress Light*, and set sail.

HULHULÉ

Arun was gazing at the twinkling lights of the ships anchored near the coast. As he watched, a bunch of lights slowly started drifting away from the rest of them.

First he thought nothing of it, but the next moment a shiver ran down his spine.

'A ship!' he shouted, pointing towards it.

Farooq whipped around, looking at where Arun was pointing.

'They're getting away!' shouted Farooq. He turned to his troops. 'Fire!'

The troops let loose their medium machine guns and Carl Gustaf rocket launchers – but the ship was out of range.

Farooq swore loudly. But all was not lost. There was another team stationed at the southern side of the island, and they were closer to the ship. They swung into action and fired three high-explosive rounds from a Carl Gustaf rocket launcher. One of them hit the steering equipment of the ship, but it still got away.

Farooq immediately sent a message to the Indian Navy. 'Keep an eye on *MV Progress Light*!'

Phase four would turn out to have a few extra steps, that's all.

THE DEADLY WEAPONS

What are all the amazing weapons that the Indian military used to great advantage in the final phases of Operation Cactus?

A medium machine gun (MMG) is mounted on a stand. It is belt-fed, that is, a long moving belt holds and loads cartridges into the gun. This is different from a rifle which is a shoulder-fired gun – and can fire only single shots.

A Carl Gustaf 84 mm recoilless weapon is an anti-tank weapon. It is lightweight, and hence portable. It is also low cost and reusable. Besides, it can make use of a wide range of ammunition.

But recoilless? How is that possible? When a gun is fired, doesn't it always recoil, that is, move backwards? Newton's Law, after all – every action has an equal and opposite reaction! You're absolutely right, and the Carl Gustaf makes use of that very law to reduce the recoil. As the gun is fired, it ejects a little burst of gas from the back, creating a forward thrust. So these backward and forward movements cancel each other out (well, almost) – and voila! No recoil!

30 mm anti-aircraft cannon: *INS Godavari* had surface-to-surface weapons and this cannon was one of them. It used 30 mm calibre ammunition (calibre is the diameter of the bullet/ammunition). This size is popular in ship weapons. It works well against armoured vehicles and bunkers, and yes, other ships, as we see in the story.

The depth charge that the helicopter dropped near the runaway ship was developed as submarine warfare. When it is dropped near a submarine or a ship, the detonation causes a huge hydraulic shock – or in other words, it results in a tremendous rush of water. The force can cause serious damage to a ship or submarine.

Depth charges have now been replaced by torpedoes. They home in on submarines and destroy them.

HULHULÉ-MALÉ

An NSS speedboat zoomed to Hulhulé to bring Farooq to the NSS headquarters. As Farooq started getting into the boat, Arun came forward too.

The tables had turned this time.

'You don't have to come, Arun,' said Farooq.

'I will.' Arun sat in the boat. And then immediately clung on for dear life as the speedboat took off at breakneck speed on a roller-coaster ride on the wild waves of the sea. After what seemed like an eternity, the boat docked at the jetty.

Farooq and Arun made their way to the NSS headquarters. Farooq was used to it, but Arun was disturbed by the scenes of violence and destruction.

They entered the NSS headquarters just as the army brought President Gayoom from the safe house.

NSS HEADQUARTERS, MALÉ

The President looked tired but was now in full command.

He greeted Arun and Farooq warmly, and placed a phone call to Rajiv Gandhi.

'Thank you for your timely assistance,' he told the PM. 'Indian soldiers are in full control of Malé.'

Rajiv Gandhi had been up all night, staying updated on the situation in Malé. He hung up and finally went to bed.

It was 4 a.m.

MALÉ

Dawn

When dawn broke again in Malé, it was with the usual comforting sounds of birdsong and the azaan.

The good news spread across Malé. The attacks were over, and the President was safe. Maldivians lined the streets, waving at the Indian paratroopers in their smart uniforms and maroon berets, cheering and clapping for them in gratitude.

The IAF was still flying in food rations and kitchen equipment for the troops, but the

troops were ravenously hungry. There were now about 1,600 troops in the Maldives, along with journalists and camerapersons who had come in on some of the IAF flights.

President Gayoom ordered that everything available at Hulhulé be provided to the Indian soldiers.

It was a Friday. The Maldives is an Islamic republic, and the President requested that the operations be called off for the day.

Farooq agreed, but he established a cordon of boats and launches all around Malé to prevent any rebels from escaping.

However, the drama was far from over.

THE INDIAN OCEAN, BETWEEN THE MALDIVES AND SRI LANKA

5 November

MV Progress Light was still at sea, about 60 kilometres off Malé.

INS Godavari was in the area returning from a goodwill visit to Australia.

'Intercept *MV Progress Light*,' the navy instructed *INS Godavari*. 'President Gayoom's request: bring mercenaries back to Malé for trial. Ensure safety of hostages on board.'

INS Betwa joined *INS Godavari*, which made contact with *MV Progress Light*. They received a message from *MV Progress Light*:

'Stay at least six miles away or we'll kill the hostages!'

But time was running out. *INS Godavari* and *INS Betwa* hemmed in on the ship. The rebels retaliated by killing two hostages.

This would not do. *INS Godavari* issued a warning. 'Surrender! Or we'll shoot.'

The rebels did not surrender. Instead, they started letting the ship's speedboat down silently, so that they could escape on it.

INS Godavari fired.

A shell from the 30 mm anti-aircraft cannon broke the foremast on *MV Progress Light.* It prised away the ship's speedboat. With that, the rebels' only hope of escape was shattered.

A helicopter dropped a depth charge. There was a massive undersea explosion. It sent a spine-chilling shudder through the rebel ship.

Some of the men panicked and jumped into the ocean.

The officials on board *INS Godavari* tried to negotiate with Luthufi, even as both *INS Godavari* and *INS Betwa* continued firing. Finally, Luthufi gave in.

Navy commandos stormed onboard.

8 NOVEMBER

INS Godavari sailed into Malé with the rescued hostages and captured mercenaries.

All phases successfully completed.

Mission accomplished.

INDIA'S SUPER SHIPS

India has one of the largest navies in the world! It has aircraft carriers, destroyers, nuclear-powered attack submarines and many more super ships.

The hero ship in this story is *INS Godavari*, a frigate, or warship. Frigates are quick and can manoeuvre easily. They escort larger ships and protect them from air, surface and underwater attacks.

INS Godavari was the first ship designed and built completely in India! The ship could launch guided missiles that could hit targets on land or sea (surface to surface) and destroy aircraft or missiles (surface to air). It could also carry helicopters on board.

Apart from Operation Cactus, *INS Godavari* took part in a number of military operations. It was decommissioned, or retired, in 2015.

INS Betwa was a frigate too, similar to *INS Godavari*, and was decommissioned in 1988, perhaps very soon after Operation Cactus. The Indian Navy currently has another *INS Betwa*, but the newbie was commissioned only in 2004.

CALL ME CACTUS, OPERATION CACTUS

The operation came to be known as Operation Cactus.

This was the first mission of its kind. A daring operation, put together with almost no information, and within just a few hours of the first SOS call. It was a groundbreaking achievement.

The crowning glory was that not a single Indian soldier lost his life!

Farooq Bulsara got his fair bit of bouquets and brickbats. As the point of contact on the ground who had to make tough decisions and with the reputation of India on his shoulders, he had a very tough job. His decision to land in enemy territory was a gamble that paid off – but it could have gone very wrong.

Operation Cactus got international praise. British Prime Minister Margaret Thatcher and US President Ronald Reagan, top military officials in Pakistan and several other countries congratulated India. *Time* magazine did a cover story on India based on this mission: 'Super Power Rising'. Another mission accomplished!

Perhaps the greatest praise for India came from Luthufi himself.

'Did you really think such a crazy, reckless venture would succeed?' he was asked in an interview.

'Why not?' shot back Luthufi. 'Anyone can be the President of such a country. If only luck had been with us. If only the Indian troops had not come for a few more hours . . .'

A NOTE ON THE AUTHORS

Sushant Singh is a journalist and senior fellow at the Centre for Policy Research. He is the author of *Mission Overseas.*

Shruthi Rao is a children's writer who has authored over ten books.

ABOUT JUGGERNAUT KIDS

Juggernaut Kids is an exciting new imprint for Indian children which focuses on inspiring non-fiction, classic fiction and beautiful illustrations. We want to create great Indian stories for today's child.

To download the app scan the QR Code
with a QR scanner app